SYMBOLS OF THE UNITED STATES

America the Beautiful

Linda Hopkins

www.openlightbox.com

AV2

Step 1
Go to **www.openlightbox.com**

Step 2
Enter this unique code
FYGIOZKHN

Step 3
Explore your interactive eBook!

AV2 is optimized for use on any device

Your interactive eBook comes with...

- **Audio** — Listen to the entire book read aloud
- **Videos** — Watch informative video clips
- **Weblinks** — Gain additional information for research
- **Try This!** — Complete activities and hands-on experiments
- **Key Words** — Study vocabulary, and complete a matching word activity
- **Quizzes** — Test your knowledge
- **Slideshows** — View images and captions
- **Share** — Share titles within your Learning Management System (LMS) or Library Circulation System
- **Citation** — Create bibliographical references following APA, CMOS, and MLA styles

This title is part of our AV2 digital subscription

1-Year Texas Subscription
ISBN 978-1-5105-8659-8

Access hundreds of AV2 titles with our digital subscription.
Sign up for a FREE trial at **www.openlightbox.com/trial**

The digital components of this book are guaranteed to stay active for at least five years from the date of publication.

SYMBOLS OF THE UNITED STATES

America the Beautiful

CONTENTS

"AMERICA THE BEAUTIFUL"

"America the Beautiful" is a patriotic song about the United States.

People sing it to show their love for their country.

"America the Beautiful" was originally written as a **poem** called **"Pikes Peak."**

A JOURNEY ACROSS THE COUNTRY

In 1893, a professor named Katharine Lee Bates traveled by train from Massachusetts to Colorado. She saw many beautiful sights on her journey.

Katharine's train journey from **Wellesley, Massachusetts,** to **Colorado Springs, Colorado,** took about **one week**.

“AMBER WAVES OF GRAIN”

On the Fourth of July, Katharine saw the wheat fields of Kansas. She called them “amber waves of grain.”

In her diary, Katharine wrote that the sight made her “a better American.”

"PURPLE MOUNTAIN MAJESTIES"

While in Colorado, Katharine went to the top of Pikes Peak in the Rocky Mountains.

She was amazed at the view of the "purple mountain majesties."

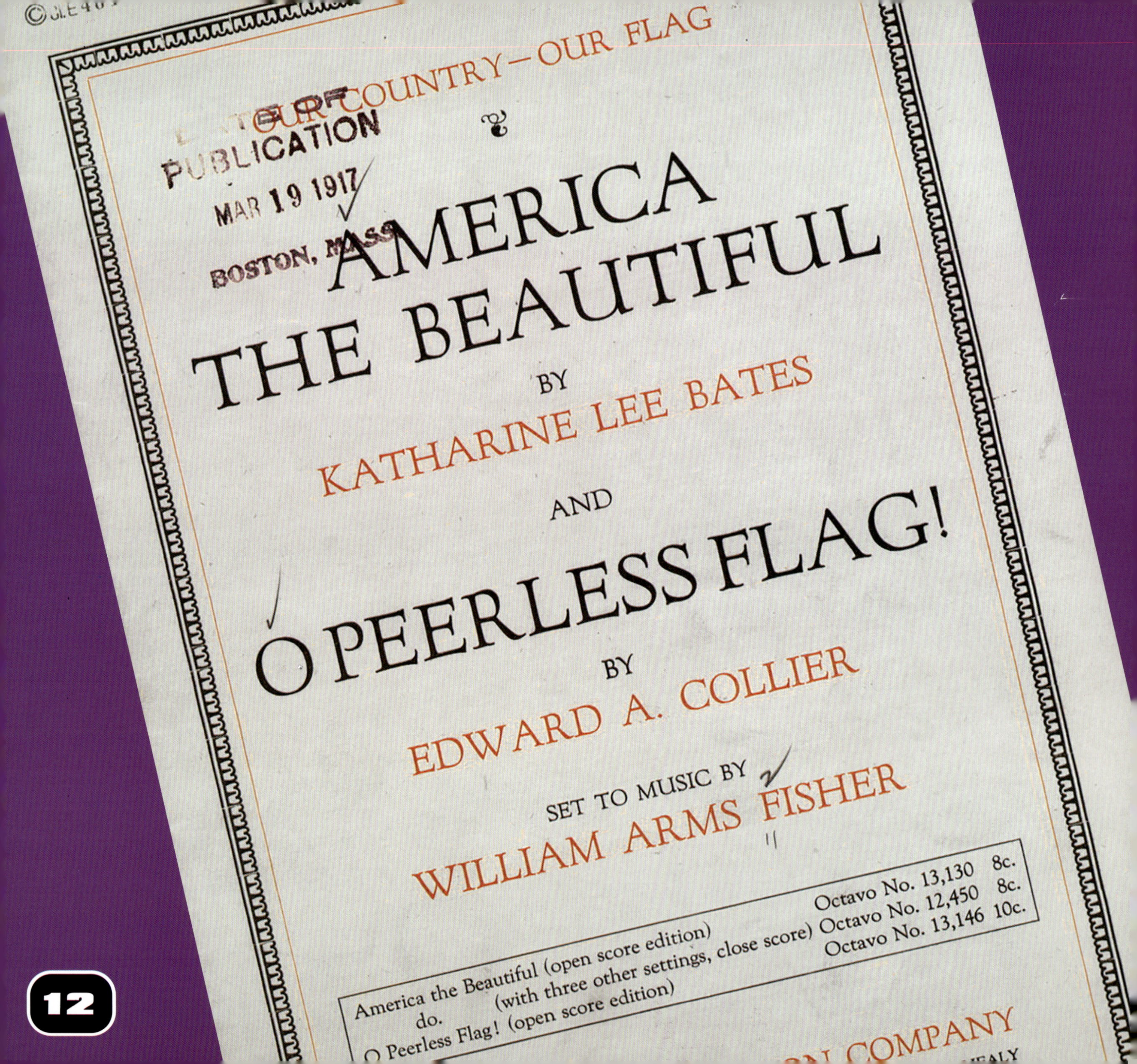
OUR COUNTRY—OUR FLAG
PUBLICATION
MAR 19 1917
BOSTON, MASS
AMERICA
THE BEAUTIFUL
BY
KATHARINE LEE BATES
AND
O PEERLESS FLAG!
BY
EDWARD A. COLLIER
SET TO MUSIC BY
WILLIAM ARMS FISHER
America the Beautiful (open score edition) Octavo No. 13,130 8c.
do. (with three other settings, close score) Octavo No. 12,450 8c.
O Peerless Flag! (open score edition) Octavo No. 13,146 10c.
COMPANY

INSPIRED TO WRITE

Katharine was inspired by her train journey and her trip up Pikes Peak.

She wrote a poem about America's beauty. Her poem soon became very popular.

SET TO MUSIC

Songs were created using the poem. One song was set to a tune by Samuel A. Ward.

This is the version of "America the Beautiful" people sing today.

Samuel A. Ward was a **church organist** in **Newark, New Jersey**. He **never met** **Katharine Lee Bates**.

A SONG FOR THE NATION

"America the Beautiful" has been printed in many books and magazines.

Americans often sing it along with the national anthem on the Fourth of July.

RESPECTING "AMERICA THE BEAUTIFUL"

People usually stand to sing "America the Beautiful."

This is a sign of respect.

"AMERICA THE BEAUTIFUL" TODAY

"America the Beautiful" is played at the Super Bowl and other sporting events.

Many famous singers have performed the song.

Rapper Post Malone sang **"America the Beautiful"** at **Super Bowl LVIII**.

SUPER BOWL

"AMERICA THE BEAUTIFUL" FACTS

These pages provide detailed information that expands on the interesting facts found in the book. They are intended to be used by adults as a learning support to help young readers round out their knowledge of each icon in the *Symbols of the United States* series.

Pages 4–5

"America the Beautiful"

"America the Beautiful" is a popular patriotic song in the United States. It was once considered as an option for the official U.S. national anthem before "The Star-Spangled Banner" was selected in 1931. "America the Beautiful" describes the natural beauty found across the United States from "sea to shining sea."

Pages 6–7

A Journey Across the Country

"America the Beautiful" was written by Katharine Lee Bates, a poet, author, and professor. She taught English literature at Wellesley College, near Boston, Massachusetts. Bates was invited to spend the summer of 1893 lecturing at Colorado College, in Colorado Springs, Colorado. Her cross-country rail journey to Colorado lasted about one week, from June 29 to July 5. Some of the inspiring sights she saw on the journey, and in Colorado, were later referenced in "America the Beautiful."

Pages 8–9

"Amber Waves of Grain"

Bates traveled through many different states to reach Colorado. On the Fourth of July, her train happened to be passing through Kansas, where she saw wheat fields stretching across the plains. Bates was deeply touched by the sight. She wrote in her diary that she was "a better American for such a Fourth." In the first verse of "America the Beautiful," her line about "amber waves of grain" refers to these wheat fields.

Pages 10–11

"Purple Mountain Majesties"

While in Colorado Springs, Bates took a trip up Pikes Peak, a nearby summit in the Rocky Mountains. After reaching the top of Pikes Peak, Bates wrote, "When I saw the view, I felt great joy. All the wonder of America seemed displayed there, with the sea-like expanse." She describes the Rocky Mountains as "purple mountain majesties" in "America the Beautiful." Today, Pikes Peak is sometimes called "America's Mountain."

Pages 12–13

Inspired to Write

"America the Beautiful" was first written as a poem called "Pikes Peak." Bates later recalled that it was while she was looking at the endless view of the Rocky Mountains that she thought of the opening lines of the poem. In 1895, two years after her trip to Colorado, Bates published her poem in *The Congregationalist*, a church magazine.

Pages 14–15

Set to Music

Bates' poem gained popularity across the country. People began setting it to the music of hymns and other songs so that they could sing it. For example, the poem was often sung to the tune of "Auld Lang Syne." In 1903, it was set to a tune called "Materna," which had originally been composed by church organist Samuel A. Ward in 1882 for the hymn "O Mother Dear, Jerusalem." This is the version of "America the Beautiful" that people sing today. Ward died in 1903, and never knew the success his tune achieved.

Pages 16–17

A Song for the Nation

Within 20 years of publishing "America the Beautiful," Bates had given hundreds of publications permission to use it. She retained the copyright to the song. However, she never charged anyone for its use and never received any royalties from it.

Pages 18–19

Respecting "America the Beautiful"

Since "America the Beautiful" is not the national anthem, there are no special rules to be observed while singing it. However, many people consider the song to be an unofficial national anthem. They stand and hold their right hands over their heart when it plays, like they do with "The Star-Spangled Banner."

Pages 20–21

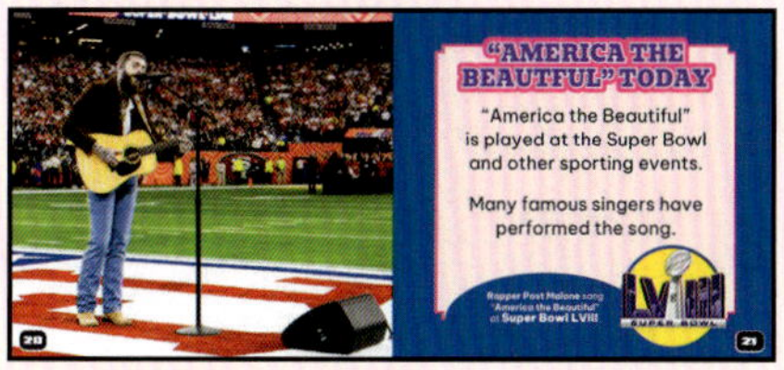

"America the Beautiful" Today

Notable singers who have recorded versions of "America the Beautiful" include Elvis Presley, Frank Sinatra, and Ray Charles. Today, the song is often played alongside "The Star-Spangled Banner" at sporting events. Mariah Carey famously sang "America the Beautiful" at the 1990 National Basketball Association (NBA) finals. Recent Super Bowl performances include renditions by Babyface in 2023 and Post Malone in 2024.

KEY WORDS

Research has shown that as much as 65 percent of all written material published in English is made up of 300 words. These 300 words cannot be taught using pictures or learned by sounding them out. They must be recognized by sight. This book contains 53 common sight words to help young readers improve their reading fluency and comprehension. This book also teaches young readers several important content words, such as proper nouns. These words are paired with pictures to aid in learning and improve understanding.

Page	Sight Words First Appearance
5	a, about, America, as, country, for, is, it, people, show, song, states, the, their, to, was
6	by, from, her, in, many, on, one, saw, she, took
9	made, of, that, them
10	at, mountain, went, while
13	and, soon, up, very, write
14	he, never, new, set, this, were
17	along, been, books, has, often, with
21	have, other

Page	Content Words First Appearance
5	"America the Beautiful," love, "Pikes Peak," poem, United States
6	Colorado, Colorado Springs, journey, Katharine Lee Bates, Massachusetts, professor, sights, train, week, Wellesley
9	diary, fields, Fourth of July, grain, Kansas, waves
10	majesties, Rocky Mountains, view
13	beauty, trip
14	church organist, music, New Jersey, Newark, Samuel A. Ward, tune, version
17	anthem, magazines, nation
18	respect, sign
21	events, Post Malone, rapper, singers, Super Bowl LVIII

Published by Lightbox Learning Inc.
276 5th Avenue, Suite 704 #917
New York, NY 10001
Website: www.openlightbox.com

Library of Congress Control Number: 2024938574

ISBN 978-1-5105-8323-8 (hardcover)
ISBN 979-8-8745-1499-0 (softcover)
ISBN 978-1-5105-8324-5 (static multi-user eBook)
ISBN 978-1-5105-8326-9 (interactive multi-user eBook)

Printed in Guangzhou, China
1 2 3 4 5 6 7 8 9 0 28 27 26 25 24

072024
100923

Project Coordinator: Priyanka Das
Designer: Terry Paulhus
Layout: Jean Faye Rodriguez

The publisher acknowledges Alamy and Getty Images as the primary image suppliers for this title.